୧୭ Coming Late to Rachmaninoff

Coming Late
to Rachmaninoff

poems by

Richard Terrill

UNIVERSITY OF TAMPA PRESS • TAMPA, FLORIDA • 2003

Manufactured in the United States of America
Book design by Richard Mathews
Printed on acid-free paper ∞
First Edition

University of Tampa Press
401 West Kennedy Blvd.
Tampa, FL 33606

ISBN 1-879852-90-X (pbk)
ISBN 1-879852-91-8 (cloth))

Browse & order online at

http://utpress.ut.edu

Library of Congress Cataloging-in-Publication Data

Terrill, Richard, 1953-
  Coming late to Rachmaninoff : poems / by Richard Terrill.-- 1st ed.
     p. cm.
  ISBN 1-879852-90-X ((pbk) : alk. paper)
  1. Music--Poetry. 2. Wisconsin--Poetry. 3. Minnesota--Poetry. I.
Title.
  PS3620.E767 C66 2003
  811'.6--dc22

                              2003014292

For Bruce Taylor,
"a sucker for the B sides . . ."

Contents

ONE

Appalachian Spring · 1
Poem in the Manner of Thelonius Monk · 2
The Moldau · 3
Monochrome · 5
My Mother at Eighty-Six · 6
Sweet Beer · 8
"Waht Does It Matter, Waht You Say About People?" · 9
November · 11
Fish/Story · 13
Chicago · 15

TWO

Once I Met B.B. King · 19
Casals · 20
Listening to Miles Davis · 21
Linda · 22
Aubade · 23
Civil Wars · 25
Lowell · 27
Point Arena, California · 29
Poker Game · 30
Stepson · 31
Unexpected Friends · 34
Three Windows · 36

THREE

Coming Late to Rachmaninoff · 41

The Center · 43

"Embraceable You" · 45

Ornette Coleman · 46

The Possibility of Love · 48

At the Lake: to a Brother before Marriage · 49

Korea Poems · 51

  Seasonal Greeting · 51

  Two Calendars · 52

  "The Azaleas" or "Azaleas" · 53

Poems after the Chinese · 55

The Accompanist · 58

Satie · 59

FOUR

The Heaven of Saxophones · 63

Flight · 65

Five Reasons Not to Play the Tenor Saxophone · 68

The New House · 69

Rise · 75

On the Radio · 77

Variations on Variations on a Summer Day by Wallace Stevens · 79

Solstice · 82

Lakeside with Sheep and Cows · 83

  Cows · 83

  Lake · 52

  Sheep Farm · 88

Acknowledgements · 91

About the Author · 93

Although our information is incorrect,
we do not vouch for it.

–Erik Satie

ONE

Appalachian Spring

We don't know where we are really, or when,
only that the instruments occur
like something not yet said. A year
newly broken from the swift red flesh

of winter, a barn newly built
on rocky confidence, allow
a brief planned carelessness
an octave deeper into the earth.

Prayer is almost comical in this abundance,
fate a minor key that's left unplayed.
This reminder courses through the woodwinds,
turns in open fields. Faith says

landscape is there. Faith and works
return *a tempo* in the greening hills,
the unmemorized lines of animals.
Pieces of sunlight cut from a cloth is sky.

It's a simple gift to know what can be taken from us.
The last time through, the piano beats time,
the cellos pray again, the preacher simply ignored,
the new Americans quiet in their house of myth.

Shakers have no descendants and therefore must have faith
in cycles of work, day and death.
No night closes over their eyes
cello and obbligato haven't foreshadowed.

Poem in the Manner of Thelonius Monk

The man standing on the airport tarmac in black and white
whirling his arms like blades of a kitchen appliance
is not a great soloist from the standpoint of technical brilliance.
He's a great soloist from the standpoint of diamonds.

The circles he turns are the sun and the moon revolving,
resolving in sky the color of blankets on a cold night.
Yes no, yes no, yes no, the stride left hand says.
"I'll have what he's having," says the melody in the right.

Some new worlds wait years for their discoverers
to get on their ships and split for Europe, metaphorically speaking;
Monk waits for the light in his brain to go green
so he can watch all those literal people cross the street at the same
    time.

Dark glasses, fedora. The air around him
is empty, by some accounts. When he plays
no one is laughing, and Monk is not so sure
they're supposed to be.

The Moldau

Smetena's piece is about a river, but all here is field
and shallow lake that spring through fall
I fish for bass,
swearing at the carp that take my bait.

It was called "program music," the idea
that music should mean, could suggest something paraphrasable—
a flowing, sparkling and blue in a Czech landscape
through the last century. In the rear view mirror

I see only enough to wonder why I've made meaning
on Blue Earth County 12, which is wholly without loveliness
and wholly without my affection, which is not to say
that I am more lovely than stalks and drifts
or that I make any sound
good enough for what they do.
(One car speaker is shot,
and the tape is crinkled where the brass come in.)

What used to be prairie is torn up
to feed us and pigs. Snowmobiles
that grind through winter, the portable
radios thudding city streets all summer
are drowned out only by the whine of my travel,
the airplane hum of Toyota pistons.
The road into snow is questions with white answers,
my vow to leave as empty as the static between radio stations
once "The Moldau" has finished flowing
and I can't take the tape out while driving an icy patch.

So I have to listen to myself blow on about southern Minnesota
while the sun sets inoffensively through a marsh of winter clouds
over the field next to the lake
or over the lake next to the field,
the field next to the field.

Monochrome

A crow and two black dogs at night,
snow falls on an ice-covered lake,
a sun worn day.
Or a blue kite against a rainless sky,
October Monday, it changes
its mind in the current.
A fire starts
and soon the trucks' new tune
channels drivers to the curb,
their faces blushed with orange surprise.

Leaves piled on leaves, maybe the man who rakes them
won't see another autumn. Maybe he knows he won't.
His jacket is torn and brown
—why buy new clothes?
Maybe this man is my father, eighteen years ago,
and I'm nowhere in the picture.
He's given up on the lawn, the yard, set his rake aside.
Sometimes he doesn't even care to read,
just sit outside when the weather allows,
prefers a chair on the cold grass
to the front porch with its concrete
sunsplashed but hard,
ringed by my mother's geraniums in terra cotta
like monuments to the summer just past,
getting the last of light,
which lengthens from above the elementary school
a little further south every afternoon.

My Mother at Eighty-Six

She's just so tired—she's been gone—
just now got back, which would explain
it, and those people who were here
have just left—not when or then
or even now. But *just*.

On the phone I tick and pause,
dependably wait, a sun locked
on the present I'm insisting on,
its bright rock. We share a talk
that makes her calm at least.
Her voice is a close guess:
*Do you want to say hello
to the other folks here? Dad?
Gramma and Grandpa?*

The past must be and must have been for her
like so many drawers in a large chest
popping out at random, unexplained
like early animation,
or steam from a calliope's pipes,
how it corresponds to pitch,
water rising to air to disappear
in a pattern other people find amusing, but too loud.

*I guess you're going to have to do
something about your mother,* she says.
She lives alone, and sees the joke
will always be on her. *I goofed up.*

But they're so near for her:
the smiling man in cocked hat and brown suit
walking toward me home for lunch, forty years ago;
the patient couple in those very old clothes
whom I danced around as they waited to die content.
What is her life with them I can't know?
I'm jealous for a moment, it arrives then passes,
and I have to play the role,
a watch too new to break.

It must be and must have been
as she told the police it was,
that her husband got off the bus somewhere
and didn't come home last night.
She thought she'd wait at least
till morning before she called,
six a.m., and could they find him
and did they think that he was gone.

Sweet Beer

The source of joy for anyone was beer.
Beer and how, aged sixteen, to get it.
My neighbor Bobby Hanrahan, two
years older, a year ahead in school,

looked like he might be 21. We'd drive
him to the Terminal Bar on Broadway
where the truckers and alchies drank,
duck down in the back seat like thugs.

All I could see was streetlight, black autumn sky.
Smooth-faced Bob drew the collar on his vinyl jacket,
lit his Lucky Strike, his look like
a young teamster. He kept us waiting there,

crouched like rodents while he had
three beers with June the bartender
—part of the M.O., he explained. The taps
were on us, as were the Luckies, and the six pack

he extorted out of the case our money bought.
The first fall snow whirled through the Broadway light.
The beer he bought tasted to us cold and new.
No other drink can taste that way.

"Waht Does It Matter,
Waht You Say About People?"

They're not shoulder to shoulder
like a high school chorus.
They've not gathered out of some
herd instinct. They've

chosen to come, all my old girlfriends,
seated as if around a table
a crew of movers has just carried away.
Their identical wood chairs slight angles askew,
the women are open before each other.
They straighten skirts, uncross jeaned legs,
kick old mud off boots. They're relaxed now,
talk show guests, and the host

never asks them about me,
but of things about them I should have known.
There is a lot of agreement and sympathy,
and after the show they order out for something:
tea and scones, or Chinese, or more beer.

One woman I cannot recognize.
She looks something like Marlene Dietrich in *Touch of Evil*
when she tells the bloated Orson Welles,
"Honey, you're a mess." She is not
my wife in a Dietrich disguise,
nor my mother, years before I was born,

nor a symbol of some unmet desire.
But the women who have stopped by this night
stare at her, quiet, intent as kites.
Outside, the moon is holding all calls,
and the trees stand darkly, avoiding mistakes.

"It just has to happen naturally," Dietrich tells me,
talking, I think, about sex, and I,
perhaps misunderstanding, say I'm fine.
I see her sad glass of a look
over one shoulder, round and motionless.
She takes one more drag on a cigarette
that never seems to burn out.

"I don't love you," she says.
Then all the old girlfriends are talking at once.

November

I

A scent is rising from the November fields,
a mixture of rain and leaf mold, a dissipating
cloud that brings joy.
Between clumps of hemlocks the ditches are full
of dead hopes, of speechless mice.
A voice of love recites
its memory of green language
at the collar and neckline of autumn.
The hearts of stones gleam like dulled silver
and the squirrels pout in the cottonwoods,
sick with distortion and hurry,
joining the dying
and their faint colors.
The joy here cannot be detected by science
or intuited by phony mystics drunk on pay
near the wharves where tourists come in.
But such a love exists as sure as this season moves
blow by blow toward winter in the chilling pools.

II

Why surprised the sun isn't around to see the end?
He's gone like music he'll play again, and we can wait.
His sky, not ours, is blank, his woods final.
The temptation not to resist conclusions
in this almost-dark
is strong.

Our ideas have leaves of their own, have hands
with the lighter flesh of palms,
upon which the gentle brush of another
can be taken as merely random.

Snow begins to fall. It's a question.
The trees move upward, scraping a low sky.
In November ground doesn't match,
the leaves bound to nothing.
Out of these woods, the dark where the sun was
seems to mean something undeniable,
winter, imagination, or just gray sound.
We've come to some conclusion about
the frailty of correspondence,
how one crow looks almost blue as he rises away,
or a fighter jet flies low, buzzing the landscape,
and we can't see the look in the young pilot's eye,
can't see if it's the look in the crow's eye
or in ours.

Fish/Story

Fish

I held the moon by both its hands.
Its body moved in an autumn stream.
Its light cast still, unthinking.

The moon climbed the bank, a curtain into the fire,
the hook deep in its broken mouth.
Its yellow rushed out like eggs.

It was that dark
and would not be light in the northwest
again this year.

Someone cut me open, a story
broken when it bellied out.

It was going to rain living arrows.
I couldn't feel anything.

Moon

There were two weeks left in the dark
when he ran line tight as a stick
through my mouth
—snagged like an arrow in both his hands.

When the yellow blood rushed out
no one was around,
and I would not be back
to tell the story.

I could feel my strength let go.
I swam deeply, climbed the bank,
a year too slow. The rain
too was warm, still alive,

but couldn't feel anything,
like sticks in autumn, like wooden gills.

My fresh belly of light
should still be thinking in the creek.

Chicago

So we limp along the Lake in Lincoln Park,
me just out of a foot cast, you
with MS, a slight case,
you say. I nod
as if that were possible,
your right hip adding
a jog you must feel to your shoulder.

Caught short by breakfast coffee we stop
next to a wall in dead vines
just past the tunnel under Michigan Avenue
where we wouldn't stop to piss
because it smelled like piss.

I tell you an article I read says cops
looking the other way at petty crime
like people pissing in the park
is responsible for the decline
of Western civilization.

Well we know that's bullshit, you say,
finishing before me.
You can often see bullshit
before I do.

If it doesn't get any worse, you say,
I'm all right,

then you talk about your wife, she
just had to have these kids
to feel complete, you said ok
and now you're getting up
in the night, in the morning
packing lunch for school,
she's at tennis with her friends
at her club she just has to have
to feel complete.

But you're a pretty good dad,
I say, and you say
you know
but we both know
neither of us cared much
years ago
about being dads.

But look, you say, it's a beautiful
day today,
you're living in Chicago, all this is here,
you gesture towards lake and city sky,
you're writing well, have enough to eat,
go to ethnic restaurants, see the Cubs.

That's right! I say and you say,
a hand to one wandering leg,

that we've just got to turn around now.

TWO

Once I Met B.B. King

Slouched in a chair, he struck me as
probably smaller than he used to be.
He didn't have that blue grimacing
smile of the album covers
—as if he enjoyed pain.
I like to remember instead, at sixteen,

rock and roll in garages, among
the trash cans and garden tools,
the neighbors gathering to listen
as pioneers might have gathered
to help build a barn—the tee-
shirt-faced kids, the young marrieds
with strollers. Years later the world

has grown comfortable on the edge of despair.
I return to the basements
to rehearse among the snow tires and
laundry tubs. Even today
among the scratchy off-season clothes,
the sensitive neighborhoods,
a little boy blocking the light
from the one basement window
bangs his plastic shovel against the glass.
His jacket and pants are forest green,
and because his mittens and cap
are red, he looks like some rare
flower growing through the frozen mud.

Casals

Though all men are brothers in the orchestra,
all men are not brothers in the world,
but this is not the fault of the orchestra.
Music is not tap water, not a bizarre costume.
Every second we live is agreement.
It hesitates only as we do; it says, *you are a simple man.*
But I am old now and this may be true only for me.
The sea rubs my cheek
like a book opened to the page of my birth.
The sea is a name: *Pau,* it says. *Pau.*
There have always been compensations.
I could sing in tune before I could talk. Do you
understand me?

Late one night Vichy France was a picture.
I walked with Gassol, the Catalan poet,
to the Abbey of Saint Michel de Cuxa.
In the sculptured darkness we rang the tower bell.
How easily the sound fell out over the valley,
diced through the narrow streets and sorrowful buildings,
rising as if from a wish: *Freedom and order. Freedom.
And order.*

Listening to Miles Davis

Someone told me once
never take life seriously,
always take yourself seriously.

Or was it, never take yourself seriously,
always take life seriously?

I imagine the middle of the night.
Not that cliché, but the real midpoint,
a blank film and the images that appear.
Sound rises up like old anger
or falls away like bitterness or salt.
Maybe winter understands something this cold
when it turns its back on its snowy audience.

The smoke in the club where he plays:
no one gets up to dance or to leave. It's 1957.
Outside, December gets polished to cold
the exact weight of a frozen river.
The point at which each note ends is irony.

I heard once that you shouldn't worry
about good ideas you get in the middle of the night:
write this, marry her, invest here.
If they're really good ideas, they'll come back to you.

Don't worry about wrong notes, Miles said.
There aren't any.

Linda

We mistook each other for unneedy people then,
two separate hands
on which no fingers were missing.

There was no groping
for neutral language. "Life," you said,
"is a war," and

"I'm not a very trusting person."
I was impressed by that: a first date
like a job interview for the Nixon administration.

One week later, your grad student apartment
was stuffed with everything you'd brought from Hong Kong
and two sons, 8 and 10.

They quickly ate their ribs and rice,
spun around the kitchen
like roaches in the light.

I was astounded that all my life
I'd never touched you.
But with the kids doing dishes in the other room,

I placed a hand on yours;
you slapped it as kindly as if
we were living in the nineteenth century.

The kids went off to bed.
Very soon it was the future
and it's stayed so ever since.

Aubade

I look at you sleeping and know
someday I will wake finally without you
who has repeated—like an alarm before the fire—
that she must go first
so as not to have to live without me.

I'll think at first that morning
that you're up early
or that I only dreamt I woke alone.
That afternoon my friends will console me
and I will pretend to hear.

I will have known for years by then
your imperfections, how your anger
came from pain, pain from outside yourself,
learned like gesture, a wrong idea, a second language,
and I'll know I'll never feel better again.

I will have laughed for years by then
about the stiff reddish way your ears
met the sides of your head
and it will not have changed
up to that day
with the rest of your beauty
which I will only remember
and my beauty
which you will have continued to imagine
as long as you could.

I will not be comforted in my grief
by you, who said that everything
would be all right, hesitating only so
I could understand that you were not telling me
that lie of immortality
but that you were with me.

After I've lost you I will still taste your body
in my mouth, your hair like light,
water and pasture.
That night walking
so many years before (it will have been by then)
we passed a field, one warm summer,
more fireflies circling over it
than stars could circle in that clear night.

Throughout our room
your clothes will be through with you, scattered,
colors that were yours,
scarves and jewelry
I will remember you wearing
as I had never noticed when you wore them,
your scent and photos,
your shoes still under tables, books hidden
intended to be read
and not now to be read by me,
stockings and boxes,
car keys, intentions,
mirrors,
your voicelessness now.

Civil Wars

The guys on the roof next door are blasting Clint Black
so I can hear it in my basement.
They're working, and working class, but Wrong.

Or a man in the paper keeps his promise
to his family, and after,
all that's left of his ex-wife's mini van
is raining down on a strip mall a half mile
away from the explosion, scraps
of their children, and hands, a glove box,
pieces of burned interior.

The long retired realtor across the street tends his perennials
and won't complain.
His wife can't remember who she is
and he'll go off again today to the home to tell her.

Some doctors left a towel inside a man
who sued and won. Children live
in buildings too dangerous to be near.

Harvey, the retired realtor, tells me
about the back deck he won't build, his plans for it.
He really likes watching the birds from there,
but how long will he live in this house, he asks me,
meaning, how long will he live?

A senator stands to say if they would only stop
building hospitals not so many people would get sick.
He poses gleaming with an ex-jock sportscaster
who will beat him in the next Party primary.

"I don't know, Harvey," I say
but not in answer to his question.
I read they have a test now
that will tell you by fifty
if you'll get what his wife has,
who can't remember her children
or why she's living now.
It's too much of a protein in the blood.

An ad on TV tells me
if I went to the hamburger chain
I could buy the action figure I saw for real
at the movies,
who wipes out rows of invaders.
I could give it to my kid, they tell me.

The old roof next door is stripped bare,
piles of shingles settling on the lawn.
The workers are gone for a sandwich or more nails,
but they've left their music on
to blast its pure bass over the neighborhood
and into the gray evening
and over the blood for sale at the hamburger chain
and the blood debated in the Senate,
and over the parking lots with their strip malls
and that blood.

My wife comes home at five
to remind me who I am.
Why am I living now?
Sik fan, she says, eat rice,
but not in answer to my question.

Lowell

At your house, still for sale, weeds gathered body high,
grass to the wheel wells of your engineless Buick.
Your lake grown over with algae by late June
so even the air was less,
like at some dacha too near an industrial park.
The scent from the cornfield across the road
made us waver. No running water
since late September,
gallon jugs for mix and brushing teeth,
showers in town at the Y.

Your past, you said, was like a solo
on some bebop re-release, sixty-five
miles an hour on bald tires without a spare.
In those days, you'd testify,
but only when asked, never a bore,
that much older than me and still
living in bars, doing your crosswords with iced tea
until lunch, then a little something. Sometimes
we spent too much time there,
or in your yard on a barbecue, slurring our thoughts,
my kids catching bullheads off your dock.
I was often too sure of what I said,
though you never let on.
You knew when not to listen
and for that people who talked too much
called you a friend.

Why is it, I asked, meaning to provoke,
all my friends are such lovable losers?

Consider, you answered,
who they have in common.

You're in a bed with the proverbial
tubes coming out of your real arms,
the date and time, city and year in literal
print the blind could see on the wall.
Why is it, I begin, and you know and begin
to tell me, but then must stop
half way, forgetting and almost
forgotten.

You were the favorite of the young waitresses,
cards you drew from a new deck
which at your touch
would melt in a glissando, fan of numbers and faces.
You saw them as they'd see themselves,
and they saw you when you were there,
and I think of you when you're not.

Point Arena, California

To a person above the beach,
drunk in tall grass out of the cold,
the stars are lighted things that move and
don't stop.
The continual fusion of hydrogen atoms,
the resulting release of energy,
the possibility of orbiting bodies, even, or life
don't matter at the end of a long road
from San Francisco.
There, the stars are hidden
in the sky everyone looks at all day:
a kid with a slapping window shade, looking,
an outfielder, a sun hissing into his glove,
the bored waiters and merchants
who might notice, walking into light,
only how the city crowds the water
and the old houses celebrate the lack of space,
obscure and unoriginal.

Poker Game

One long sleeve torn at the end,
the other folded back—no aces hidden there—
he drinks his cream soda, smokes the clear air,
and bets and raises like a shark in a bad western
and not like my stepson in our Saturday night game.
His mother is the third player, who will fold
with a high two pair; his teen brother too old
for this, over some cliff on TV in the den.
He takes one card, wants it red,
and not filling his flush, says
"Mom, you're breaking my hearts,"
and proud of his pun, he gleams
like a needle finally free of its thread,
like the idea that was his.

Stepson

I

They egged your car again on Saturday night:
the run down trap I gave you, with half a gas tank,
heater that only works on high, doors
that won't lock (when will the thugs find that?)
and a windshield crack across the passenger side
where I banged a piece of lumber against the glass
loading through the hatchback. Do they come

every weekend because of the car you drive
too fast (maybe to compensate for its junkiness),
because you're straight A's and a little smaller,
don't as clearly wear your insecurity
(you can tell them to fuck off without
having to say so)? Or do they come because,
Chinese, you still don't look American to them?

It bothers me that it bothers you
less than it bothers your mother
who's bothered less than I am.
You're used to the teen politic
of group and soul, the many and the one
trying to find a many he can stand.
No role model, I tell the cops again,

a race-based crime, my urge to take a bat
to the vandal's hood and lights, the cops saying even then
the shattered glass doesn't prove anything when
the kids say they were hanging at the dance,

nowhere near a dozen eggs which drip
like question marks along the driver's side.
I almost wish they'd spray paint "Chink pigs die"

so I could raise a stink in our churchie town.
You sleep in again, are late for church,
where you'll usher, meet your friends.
You take the bucket and sponge
scrape away again the trail of gold,
a hardened morning sun.

II

Nobody can tell you.
Only you know.

Nobody can tell your
drawn window shade and chaos closet.
You've arranged the space
in your empty drawers
to accommodate the clutter
on the desk, shelves, and floor.

You have a father
and he's not here, has never been.
I don't need to tell you
you are living in my house.

Others might be jealous of the certainty
with which ideas occur to you
before you doubt them,

such sure knowing
and later emptiness.

An actor can make himself understood
playing the part of a boy or man
who does not understand himself.
You have made that speech and
you will make it.

Only you know
your language, a book,
two fathers, missing from the shelves
and no one can tell.

Unexpected Friends

Old lilacs decrescendo on a kitchen stand,
placemats in a stack,
numb late romantics on the radio,
and clouds that move in like bad neighbors
who clear away the confusion in the yard the cardinals liked.
Bowling trophy in with the antique candleholders—unused—
and the Master's diploma—unused.

You'll find my house the way I find it mornings,
couch and chairs a file for packs, papers,
books stacked according to degree unread,
dust undisturbed, dishes at peace with themselves,
bedsheets random, forgotten their story.
Popcorn popper, unanswered letters,
shook rugs on a rail,
and lots of newspapers
and not much news.

I like unexpected friends who come by
play a note then drive off.
We make plans as if tomorrow were today.
We have a drink or don't, don't notice
the pauses in talk,
soloists with a missing page.

The shovel they came to borrow, unborrowed,
the connections between things in the world
seem once again to exist.
I defect from the study

to watch their car back off,
wave like some doubled consonant
before an ending.

Three Windows

One crow flies from left to right across the panes,
flies, for this is a changing picture, in motion
like the cars on the highway out there too,

rolling more surely toward scrap.
The grandest of the trees has risen in the far right pane
over the years, since before there was a house

or a window through which to see it. Now we see
what would be its waist,
a black and furrowed

implication
of a hundred branches, each
tapering to its single point. For these

are winter trees against north light. Oaks mostly,
each locked on a path to light
that changed slightly

with the turns and growth of other trees.
A few leaves remain, this late in the season.
Not pennants or flags, they make

no flap in this strong wind
seen not heard inside:
these few inevitable conclusions

left unchallenged, uncommented upon
this morning when the north
sky is a mottled gray. Light

swings right to left
above the frame and out of view,
and brown fields and pale grass ending.

Then suddenly another road
that hadn't existed until driven upon,

a red pickup at an angle through what's left of corn
toward the main road
that leads to town.

THREE

Coming Late to Rachmaninoff

Sergei, I'm forty-three and I've learned to love.
It's middle age, I know.
When we recognize the power we never had
—a post-Romantic flurry of notes and emotion—
is declining. And so I'm driving

past the K-mart, the older part of the new
strip development, Sergei, some holiday
or other, lights screaming in a sky,
pennants at a car lot calling,
and the balding salesmen smile.
"To hell with them," you once said, "I don't know how
to write a symphony."

But I put on my Toyota's warning flashers,
pull to the curb to cry
at the adagio of your Second try.
Among the wrappers and crap from convenience stores,
shards of broken glass like clarinets,
is that theme we scoffed at younger,
da da da DEE da dum,
the styrofoam cups outlasting even the strings,

and nothing changes by your music
except that I am changed.
I walk to the median listening, the traffic passing
while the violins climb your dominant chord
to its beautiful resolution.

You of the passionless melancholy
who thought himself "a most uninteresting man,"
who wept a little daily, a black well.

The Center

*"Emily Remler Dies
Of Heart Attack
On Australian Tour;
Jazz Guitarist Was 32"*
—New York Times

One night in a bar I listened,
your notes hard swung, quietly smart, barely enough,
in case the next chorus might say more,
that luxury of progress and resistance.
The space between notes appeared
like bits of time,
but now time is a machine, and it's broken.

What tense to use for those who've never been
in our lives—who can't judge us, just
as we can't judge. Hearing you
only one night I thought we might have had
something to say to each other.
Such small grief for a stranger goes away
only to reappear for myself,
my life, too, become a yes or a no.

Unaccustomed, we listen with our eyes, see
a body slackened, almost limp
as if in escape through good pain.
Closed thin smile,
nod of the head to applause,
understatement given to periods of music,
your not quite knowing.

Maybe we know only the titles:
All Blues, Hot House,
Softly as in a Morning Sunrise.
And we know that silly slang,
outside, yeah, good groove,
we think musicians use
to avoid saying something.

The heart is the center
but I thought for you the hands,
their quickness in what I imagined was their tenderness,
their music begun to age and change
now young and gone.

"Embraceable You"

In the first version, Billie's voice sounds like what will be left
tomorrow in a glass of Scotch today. It's half drunk and set next
to the moon shining irreplaceably on a table on a nice veranda in a
plain hotel, long ago in Harlem. You leave the room for a sandwich,
walk out while the sax player takes a ride and Billie rests. By the
out chorus I think I know what Billie means by "naughty baby." I
change the record while you're gone.

"Do you want anything?" you call from the open refrigerator light.
"Come to me do," I whisper.

And in the next version, Nat Cole's piano sounds like the affairs of
his own black tie. There's no veranda this time, but a drummerless
moon is tipsy for a few too many bars. You've come back like a
gypsy—with two tall beers and no glasses. The chorus, too, repeats.
Nat sings about your many charms. "Miss me?" you ask.

In the last version, I answer, you never left at all. Sinatra wears
his hat even in the studio, we see from the album cover. He's
overproduced but irreplaceable. The strings behind him are sheer
as the moonlight we don't have to imagine streaming in our small-
town old-house bay window on a very, very cold night. You huddle
to me as if we were still not married. "I like this one best," you say,
my arms about you as you turn the music off, and the lights too,
and disappear.

Ornette Coleman

In 1957 he was a wing without a bird.
Hands like an elevator operator's, he found a streak
down the middle of luck, a corner to turn with music
more important than stopping on every floor
for all the same old notes.
It's as if the coroner had died, as if

he said you could just make it up,
melody and harmony the difference
between worn leather and an old shoe.
Later, his pupils were everybody who listened

and played: Coltrane went through his apartment
opening all the windows at night, and Sonny Rollins
locked the door and didn't talk to anybody.

He was as notorious as a missing page, a kid with a violin
in a machine gun case.
But exactly sixty-seven miles north-northwest

of the Five Spot Cafe in New York that fall
that Ike's heart again fluttered the nation to panic
there was still a woods
they've since cut down for a nursing home and
fast oil change place.
In fifty-seven the hardwoods were thick as matches,
ready to light themselves into a fire
nobody else had thought of.

By the late sixties Ornette was working
as a ticket taker on the New York subway system,
his music evoking fear inside the record jackets
where it mostly lived by then.

You paid your money, and you got on the train.

The Possibility of Love

occurs to us like a new color,
like the idea to write a letter,
occurs like the morning of the accident.

The possibility of love rises like a blanket
shook out after a day at the beach.

The possibility of love is a child.
It's spring in the mind of one red bird.

Other possibilities make you stop and go.
The possibility of love is a working vacation.
It's a campaign without a manager,
a campaign with no election,
it is no campaign at all.

In Wisconsin in the 1950's,
wives in long jackets and bright work dresses
ran damp cloths along clotheslines.
Blue clouds blew by.
What the wives hung out to dry
was the possibility of love.

At the Lake: to a Brother before Marriage

As she steps from the car I see her
as she is, the withered legs
of palsy, the stooped back—how she wants
no help around the mud and water
that have settled in the driveway—
the way she grasps your hand.

For a moment I watch my hands
stutter and shake, then look to hers
—the same—yet I look away
not to stare at the legs
which do not do what she wants
but tremble and waver like water.

We walk through the yard to the water
at an uneven pace. The sun is a hand
that smooths the lake and shore. The willows want
to grow together. The sapsucker waits for her
mate on the backhouse, then wings away.
You offer cheese and the chipmunk climbs your leg.

We settle into chairs with beers; the legs
bow some with our weight. Near the water
our women lie. We half-talk in the way
we did as roommates, our hands
turn circles, not saying what we want,
then you speak: "I'm myself with her,"

"I'm going to marry her,"
and then the plans, the money, how her legs

are getting stronger with work; you'll want
a family. Forgive me: I imagine whiskey and water,
you at bedtime, not wanting to go, the way
you must lie with her, how you place your hands.

She struggles to us and clasps your hands.
You rise, you lean against her.
She will not back away,
but braces lightly against the legs
of the largest willow. *What I want,
this is what I want*—you walk to the water.

Legs that walk at all can walk away.
With my voice of water, I say what I want:
brother, let your hands hold each step of her.

Korea Poems

Seasonal Greeting

Now the pine boughs are bowed with the sad weight
of winter's children and the sun seems far
from our homes and lives. This
is the way we might begin a letter to
or from Korea, the writer's object
to see how new a way
he can describe the season—the weather
as he looks out a window, or if it's dark
some internal weather
that might be good written down.
The sun lowers itself
out my window and I'm afraid
I haven't written a word—it's not
indecision wound down to silence,
just the enormity of things: darkness
and other than darkness;
gravity and the idea of light and air;
the man bagging at the grocery store whom I talk to
because he talks to me and I like it.
There's starting at the beginning of the story, in the middle
of the threat of the ongoing, that is,
a pine tree heavy with snow at the end
of a short day, when kids go home from school.

Two Calendars

On one kind the pictures change,
the past months tucked behind the future,
a fox in alders become two woodpeckers
on a bare branch, or in an old Korean scene
the pigtails of running boys
flying just as kite tails did
the month before. We can look back far
to see a dog and children on a winter lake
or ahead to see boys with tops
(one leans close on hands and knees
to hear its whir). This spring month those children
might help in the fields; one rushes
a blossom to his mother and the neighbor,
busy pounding laundry on the bank of the stream
below the waterwheel flanked by cherry trees, newly bright.
On another kind of calendar
the months are torn away.
The picture stays the same, become only more worn
in its place on the kitchen wall.
A red tree is straining to match the sky, and a pheasant
stands on a single rock, almost green.

"The Azaleas" or "Azaleas"

"When you go," "If you go" begin two translations
of the great poem by Kim Sowŏl,
whose azaleas, which burn in version A,
are gathered twice on a green mountainside, or perhaps a hill.

Are the famous flowers in armfuls or in another measure, unspecified?
Is she *through with him*, or just *sick and tired*
is what choice we're left as the poet,
that lover who bids good-bye quietly
or without a word,
is left, we conclude, with emptiness.

Some evenings in her dim office we translated
the minor poets—Mi Kyung, with her dictionary,
her desk light a yellow island,
me with pacing coffee about to make
art out of the least utterance, out of
the brown creaking of her dusty chair.
Mostly her voice became soft
when she began to read
her finished drafts: title first,
inflection dropping in lyric pain—a cultural obsession—
followed by a dark pause for stillness:
"Spring Night"   "Paper Kite"
"To the Wind"   "Musky Scent"
"Rainy Day". . . . She was afraid, she said,
it would not sound the same or right in English.

But it's all I can know, the translations, and so today
I will not weep or show tears,
perish or die, but want
to scatter, strew azaleas in her path
before her light, soft, gentle, gentle step.

Poems after the Chinese

The wind blows rain
and soaks my basement office.
My wife runs the lawnmower
into a fire hydrant. Here's the bill.

A hungry crow caws above the wooded ravine
below my window.
Kids build forts in there,
the confusion of branches.

See those empty bottles
beside my desk?
Those scraps of paper that were
once in a pile?

Others are worse off than I am.

***

What to do with all those old jazz LPs,
like an orchard in the wind
full of fallen petals?

Herbie Hancock still lives in his city of instruments,
his music a moving field I walk through.
Chet Baker's jade-white pictures tell us

the quality of the wine
is not the quality of the story.
Not always.

John Coltrane plays in a deep woods
inside which days pass, unnoticed.

***

All afternoon the streetlights glow.
In late October the sun is a traveler
useless to long for.

I think I'll go out and rake the leaves
I raked yesterday.

***

Car horns blast in a row
after a wedding.
Headlights come on
in the other lane
like twin moons that don't have to rise.
They peer into darkness I've passed.

***

To my lover I grant my failure,
which is like love.
It takes too long to get to know
its nature.

After his long phrase
we can hear
the flutist take a hollow breath.

The curtains flap open and closed
and scent from our flower bed reaches us
between wrong notes.

***

Beethoven's Eighth didn't get the raves
of his Seventh Symphony.
But it was pretty good.

In the city park the black puddles
that used to be raindrops,
the red beer cans overflowing a green trash basket,
the list of cars in the lot
are all things I've seen.

I've never cared so little about a place
I was so reluctant to leave.

The Accompanist

He listens for birdsong
or in town
the street sweepers, air brakes
car horns with their overtones
buses that pass without
any people on them
the afternoon sun that changes

He doesn't need to hear the missing part
finds form in what recurs
without having sounded first alone
echo without a call

She gestures for his bow
which he takes the short way
a stone skips across water
away from shore, mostly flight

He practices silence for her
major then minor
turns pages on a stage
like leaves that rest
on the path through the park
before the sun is up
and no one has walked there yet

Satie

Sometimes music is only furniture
in which we rest in our dirty clothing;
sometimes the clothing is clean, but trying to listen,

we're no less perfect a burden to the notes,
leaving our shape in the cushions,
the unseen oil from the back of our head,
sheen on the dark antimacassar.

At twenty-one he left the *conservatoire*
to become a café pianist.
One year, we're told, he locked the door

and let no one in.
The chords of his sarabande
were fruit in a bowl of twilight.
He thought art shouldn't mean anything,

and so others studied that
until they weren't certain.
What is the relationship of the self to a glass of water?

Take away the glass and have only the water.
Take away the water and have only the thirst
until the body is weak,
until the hands blur in practice at the keyboard,

the lines around the eyes deepen.
One year he let no one in.
Sometimes music leaves us lost,

the way one in the woods doesn't choose
a particular path through the trees,
but merely hopes he'll get home. I'm listening
to Satie's "Three Pieces in the Shape of a Pear,"

music smaller
and rounded at one end
from which a core extends

and a brown
leaf waves lightly as a flag.
The four hands on the keys
belong to the same soul,

its residue sticky, minor, and sweet.
At fifty-nine he left the *conservatoire*
penniless, as that story goes,

a counterpoint he studied
that he insisted didn't mean anything,
mocking those upstarts with their suspensions
and quick-sand harmonies.

He insisted one last piece
be played with chords light as a floating egg.
Others were not certain.

Once he sent Picasso out to find
an airplane propeller he'd scored in a ballet.
To Cocteau he assigned a typewriter, a ticker tape,
and a siren that rose like a bird.

FOUR

The Heaven of Saxophones

My boss, she's there. My mother,
she's there too.
My elementary school teachers,
even Miss Parliek, never married herself,
"his hand writing...*still*," she always reported.

My dentist, she's there. That cheerleader
at the homecoming dance, thirty-two
years ago. That woman on the train that time
not knowing to this day that I exist.
Sheila's there, who ran off to São Paolo
with the Brazilian cardiologist. And so

we do a bossa nova: "Triste," "Meditation," "O
Grande Amor," by the second chorus of which
the moon is shining in the room,
the drinks are sad and the walls sigh.

Jodi's there, and Akemi. Marta, and Mary,
Jeanne, Mi Kyung, and all the names I've given them
are given again and not taken back.
"Thanks," I tell the crowd
after a tender ballad.

The bass player diddles,
the drummer taps a tentative something
—they've been ready all their lives.
We go into "Autumn Leaves," a moderate up.
A diminished scale falls across the first two bars.

My sound is breathy, breathless with air.
The reed is damp like good mold. I like especially
the bridge, the relative minor
reminding us it's there, as in the part of life
that's not music.

Flight

At Wal-Mart in my town, in a bin
with Mantovani and Mitch Miller,
Charlie Parker blows another chorus of "Crazeology."
The tape's so cheap it kinks up
in my box when I get it home,
the auto-reverse kicks in in the middle of Bird's ride,
and suddenly the out chorus of "Quasimodo" blares tinny
through my bookshelf speakers, the "b" side. And then another wrinkle
and we're back to Parker's solo again, the same licks
we just heard. It's said

Bird never repeated an idea.

There was a time in my life I didn't like bebop.
There was something wrong with me. I thought
music should move slowly enough that I could hear,
this before days like today
when I came home from work
and blew hard bop licks during the noon hour
on my tenor sax in the basement.
Before I liked bebop I thought most phenomena
could be explained.

The tape's cover art is an old black
and white photo, Bird's slouched frame cut out and tinted
in primary colors. His eyes
bulge as if caught in a lie, his shirt hot pink
and tie mottled blue.

There are no liner notes. Who are the other players?
Diz? Max Roach? My Aunt Mildred? Who
on the live tracks
like "Marmaduke" or "Groovin High,"
which burn like lit fire,
who are all those people talking
in the background?
Why aren't they listening, in this unnamed club
to this unspecified rhythm section
in this world never quite identified enough?
The gray sheet of their conversation thrown over the art
is like a second drummer
with a sizzle cymbal and a tendency
to rush a little.
I can hear glasses clank, voices compete
for attention.
Somebody's trying to pick somebody up
back there in 1948,
and I can almost hear his car pull away on 52nd Street
in the rain. I hope he got lucky. And the guy

who just came in—double-breasted seer sucker suit,
the kind I would have worn—
who can't get the bartender's attention, who's mad the band's on break,
who just ended an argument with his wife
the way they always end
when somebody stops talking,
and so he stopped for smokes, came in the back,
passed a bloated black man lighting up a joint in the alley,
holding a soft-sided suitcase the size of an alto saxophone,

and going on about Stravinksy,
Bartók, and Henry Wallace. "Who in the hell
the angry husband asks, "is that Negro?"

Five Reasons Not to Play the Tenor Saxophone

Its shape curved like grace turned back
on itself is like lost love

Its green brass lake and oil smell
remains all night on your hands

The cold mouth piece you must blow
into with an o of the
lips as one blows into a
fist on a cold afternoon
often produces music
you hadn't thought of before

The reed you must hold up to
light to see its cane heart—if
you put it in your mouth and
try to talk no one will know
what you are trying to say

The flowers etched in lacquer
on the gold bell

The New House

1. Arranging Furniture

The recliner in the corner
for the light and a view
of the garden. The black chest
with inlaid mother of pearl,
four women (or is it two twice?)
who curl white sleeves around shoulderless
bodies we assume are also white.
Up against the wall with that.
Maybe a rocker near the fire.

It's 3 a.m. I've just begun.

Except there's no garden to see from here.
Compost molders at the foot of the lot,
a suburban lawn and line of shrubs
marking the end of one fiefdom and the beginning
of where the neighbor has to mow

and beyond that a street and beyond
another lawn and beyond—all the way
to a freeway too crowded to drive
and a mall where nobody goes,
and another and another. Well,

you can't see that either at this hour,
AC rumbling like a truck down our new street,
night a black dog that will

turn a circle twice, curl back
the same place on the bed.

Grandpa's Atwater Kent?
Try it next to the spinet piano;
the vase of African violets
will hide the spot the finish cracked.
Out the window are thatch and weed, patches
of creeping charlie in the shade—as if I put them there.
The strip mall and mini mart,
they've been set out of sight but not mind.
Pointlessness and despair
over that worn spot in the rug.
That second nightcap down in the basement.
The crashed hopes and fractured plans,
we'll decide later, so leave them in the packing crates.
And the potted palm, will it be happy
so far from afternoon light?

2. Closing

The former owner's wife died in this bedroom.
He told me before closing—thinking that Chinese like my wife
would see an omen in that.   My wife laughed,
said to thank him, but I forgot: the weather
had been sweltering, a football player
died from heat, and I was worried
about my movers keeling over,
boxes, vans, inspections.
No time for ghosts.

She'd been a lean figure on the block, the late Mrs.
running by, long-legged first steps of her daily miles,
and a tender mother, so the new neighbor later
told me.   She worked out of the home,
not fifty, then liver cancer (she never drank)
stilled her in a year.
She'd manicured her flowerbed, cared for it
like her children, watched it
from her desk—which her husband left for me,
too old and big and not-antique to move.
I write there now and watch the yard she saw.

It's not a deal breaker, I joked when he asked
about my wife's beliefs, then thought perhaps
I'd spoken in bad taste.   But we shook hands and the flowerbed,
the bedroom, the house weren't his anymore.

For the next seven nights my wife
would light a joss stick
and plant it in a drinking glass—our best set,
one glass to each entrance to the place
(what spirits, I wondered, would come and go
through the garage?). It was the Chinese way,
not *feng shui*, not religion, but some practice
I'd never seen before, thus felt surprise.
Four doors, four glasses,
and each morning
the broken snake of ashes on the floor.

Karen, she'd said each night,
but not out loud, not for me to hear,
I know you were a good person. You're still
in this house. That's ok. Your family isn't here.
You can go to them.

The eighth day, the long hot spell broke,
and I weeded the perennial bed,
watched it from my desk
the rest of that summer and fall,
and past the first frost.

3. How not to live there

The way a stout man will come
to resemble his pet, the way
married people grow to resemble
each other. The way, kids
gone and extra weight around the belt,
the happy, slower couple decide to get
a dog, one too chicken

to stay outside in winter,
scratching at the patio door to come in,
to be around people or sit by the gas fireplace,
or maybe sit in the wife's lap
(the dog, not the husband)
on Sunday afternoons, the NFL
blazing away on sixteen stations.

I'm glad it's over, the angst
of my twenties. How silly young people are,
trying to get laid and failing or not,
never somehow enough, all wanting to be artists,
living off Daddy's trust (like me, not an artist,
and not much money passed on), or failing
that, TV anchors, or mavens of international

trade. I'm hoping in twenty years
today will seem more important
than twenty years ago seems now. Today

I put the storms on, pruned the vines,
looked for a deal on something to buy
for the new place without spending
too much time in the car.

The way some drivers in my new city, cut off
or followed close behind
will hoist the finger and a barrage
softened only by the windshield.
Today I will laugh, make faces
at offenders as they pass,
maybe blow a kiss.

Rise

You're wearing your gold pendant,
the Chinese character for "Thanks,"
which is what your name meant before you left Hong Kong.
It's over your Georgetown Hoya sweatshirt
the kids wouldn't wear
because it signified gang affiliation
in the small town in which we no longer live,
where there weren't any gangs.
Middle-aged, we wear a lot of hand-me-ups
and put the money we save on clothes
into church bonds, growth and income funds
that lately don't grow and don't give income.
You just got up, Saturday,

and against that blue shirt with its
dull white lettering cracked from the dryer,
you still have on
the salmon sweat pants,
and your dark-framed glasses you found on rising, pre-contacts,
the ones I say make you look like Madame Mao Zedong,
known to her frightened subjects as "the white boned demon,"
and the plastic slippers you wear to the garage,
unlikely Cinderella with the week's recycling.

You've been sleeping late;
I like writing poems about that,
secrets I'll soon tell:

the fights our fights,
the day ours too.
I'm in the basement,
you warm upstairs in the bed,
a story about ourselves
that I'm imagining true.
Then in a moment you rise,
ask me what I'm doing down there,
do I want rice soup, or should we walk.
Later, we'll do your taxes, and see what we owe.

On the Radio

*"I wrote my answer about my parents dying in the same year,
one in the spring and one in the fall."*
—Cecil Smith, age 94,
oldest known recipient of a GED

I wonder what the question was,
and what those in charge,
suits and ties in Central Office,
those who studied education hard but hated
to teach and couldn't say so,
what they expected the young people to answer,
1. In 500 words, why did you quit school?
2. What is the worst thing that can happen to someone?
3. What did you learn from experience
you could not have learned in school?

The inflection of the interviewer rises and falls,
peaks and valleys of condescension.
She talks as if he understood
a different language
(he does, though not the one she speaks).
It was the kind of feature they run ten minutes
before the news, public radio
finding novelty, reaching
beyond New York to the provinces.
Her voice climbs the ladder of the slide
then starts down the waxed way.

"What's next for you, Mr. Smith, a dorm room at UCLA?"
"Well, keeping good health, I imagine."

4. In eighty years or less, describe
one unimaginable sorrow. Be vague,
general, and philosophical. Cite examples
only from your own experience, feeling free
to ignore the reading selections from your test packet.

5. Have you ever felt bad about an experience
and later realized you shouldn't have?
If not, explain.

Variations on Variations on a Summer Day
by Wallace Stevens

1

Being, for old men, time of their time,
they watch, delicately as they think women do,
while beautiful collies walk with women masters,
cut across the corners of their lawns.
Yes, the old men feel themselves, as sun
shines on the subjects from under a threatening evening cloud.

2

Say of the house that it was standing
next to the man in plaid pants
who was trying to sell it.

3

Into the sea,
into the belief,
into the hidden vein
the stick divines is there,
into the open spaces car windows were
comes the rain.

4

It was not yet the hour to be dauntlessly leaping:
look at
the children's bikes, lying still,
kick stands piercing air,
handlebars like the skull of a steer,
bike on its ribs, like summer,
rich with abandoned plans.

5

As a boat feels when it cuts blue water,
at last most perfectly alone.

6

As you improvise on the piano,
the tyrannical effect of a distant rehearsing
marching band,
tin sound of horns like early television,
the random banging of drums,
seems to interfere.

7

In objects such as white this, white that,
so the summer colors wish to be left alone
until night, when they can wear their night disguises.

8

In light blue air over dark blue sea
the painter finds a reason for his afternoon.
The wind he can't record ripples his canvas
and from the schoolhouse that he paints
children fly like sparks
in the last century. Tonight,
my eyelids that close upon your image
are like twin dark skies.

Solstice

wind rose like a low horn
on one note and the dark green sound
didn't pass as much as glow

we huddled in a human way
the reason we came to this place
foot in another shoe

our act of only seeing
our turning sight declined like a fence
into the horizon

where we knew a river locked
an ice dry house
we were alive

under the bell of wild sky
and flew deeper
into the woods how much

can we gain how much
we love to lose to this cold
garden under a hard snow

once in each school of days we note
this long hem of night
its good and simple movement

all ablaze with stars we won't remember
please answer the following
will it come again

Lakeside with Sheep and Cows

Cows

Adagio sostenuto

The Holsteins have survived their day of grass.
They climb the odd evening hill
in a pasture not like a park.
From their gaze a line of cold must pass.

From their nostrils breath returns to air.
The lake is a flat place, beyond, sometimes bright,
sometimes gray-green to match the other shore;
water is an old bathtub half inside the fence.

They can't recognize beech, oak,
moss cover, ivy-wound trunks.
The cows appear to be moving,
up the hill and down.

And they are moving. They have perhaps
not awakened from their walking sleep.

intimissimo

A black cow nuzzles another's neck,
their feet too small for their stocked bodies.
One cranes to the low branch of a leafless tree
(for this is early April),

another scrapes a head against bark.
They descend in the same line, but not the same order.
The air that follows them flows away;
they make no sound that can be heard

from beyond the clusters of daffodils
(which they ignore, which ignore them),
from past the barbed wire and the gravel path, the lawn,
the porch, the front door or south-facing window.

They seem to be asleep but never are,
not like children playing, or children sleeping.

allegro agitato

I admit I'm watching them,
though I'm no farmer and drink little milk,
have never touched them and wouldn't now.
The cows resist description,

become their black and white,
eyes dumbly open as if interested in shapelessness.
One scratches a leg with another leg, like a dog.
They dance and butt slowly, tails swish air,

a confident amble all an act.
I'm seeing them move within the frame
of my south facing window, second floor,
and have taken this time

to describe their deliberation,
the tearing out of grass I could hear

if I drew closer, down the stairs
and out to a verdant river wider than the world
I can imagine for them.

Lake

accelerando

The end of the short pier groans
like a wooden mattress
a half beat past the moving water,
the middle submerged
and wavering in six inches of clear black.

To the right, tips of green
show above the patterned surface:
waves of darker black, their angle
determined by contour, weather, and depth.

A bee states his peace near my forehead;
tree roots jut from the small salvation
of earth packed hard a foot or so above the water.
The roots curl and make shape of themselves
into the air and then the water.

Spit-white foam rides the surface at shore
and an old tin can is rusted at its base,
misshapen at its reddened lip.
Was it used to bail a boat, not here now

next to the empty boathouse?
One duck cricks then dives.

It's stunning how little color plays here:
the light gray of the table-level surface,

the darker gray of the other side
that I call green because I know it to be,
not because I see it that way now.

Water walkers have appeared, from where?
They can give no reason
for their directions and angles,
black seeds on a still dark cloud.

The end of the t-shaped pier is concrete block
reinforced with steel, and bolted wood.
Clumps of grass growing between slats
are like clumps of beach grass, islands in sand.
The distance between me, who tries to observe,

and that which I see
is like the distance between me and other observers.
What we see is finally within us, what prevents us from seeing,
colorless and shape changing, form-changing:

the modulating pitch of a small plane
out of sight above cloud cover.

Sheep Farm

tranquillemente

My footsteps on dry grass
send them scattering, of one mind
and one body off-white, head to head.

The seven sheep stand so close
that the rest of the world
outside this fence is diminished by them:
one moving whitish rock
in an Irish Zen garden.
Can they hear me thinking

above the spiritual noise the sunshine makes
in a dry April? Sometimes
there's snow this late, the housekeeper said.

Axel the brown neighbor dog
stands pointed toward the brush,
some distant ancestor in his mix
telling him to do so. He gives
up on me finally, seated in one place,
our walk apparently over.

For I'm here with my notebook, sketching sheep.
If it's good enough for the brush and easel crowd,
why not a pen and paper man?
I see each black, nose-prominent face,

rippling jaw content with grass,
unimportant eyes I can't make out from here.

I draw one white fur body with stepping stool legs
lost six paces from the others,
a sun to their clouds, a change to their weather.

I can't ignore the lake beyond,
that gray silver band aligned on the horizontal:
road—grass—fence—grass—sheep—*lake*—hill—sky.
Across the lake a car door
cracks closed through
the bee buzz and bird whistle

and blank wind through leaves of rhododendron and holly.
Some sheep bleat and baa, but from another pasture out of sight.
I wait for the driver to bait a hook lakeside,

become only a man
fishing. The dog's snout is on my page.
He sees scent and not the coming evening.

ACKNOWLEDGEMENTS

I thank the following journals in which poems in this collection originally appeared, often in different forms: "Monochrome," "Once I Met B.B. King," "Fish/Story," and "'Waht Does It Matter, Waht You Say About People?'" in *Another Chicago Magazine (ACM)*; "Coming Late to Rachmaninoff" in *Ascent*; "November" in *Books Ireland*; "Appalachian Spring" in *Crab Orchard Review*; "Lakeside with Sheep and Cows" in *Cream City Review*; "Seasonal Greeting" in *From the Tongue of the Crow: Wisconsin Review Anthology*; "Variations on Variations on a Summer Day by Wallace Stevens" in *Hayden's Ferry Review*; "Poem in the Manner of Thelonius Monk," "Ornette Coleman," and "Embraceable You" in *High Plains Literary Review*; "Three Windows" in *Hubbub*; "The Moldau" in *Iowa Review*; "Civil Wars" in *Laurel Review*; "Listening to Miles Davis" in *Midwest Quarterly*; "Two Calendars" and "At the Lake: to a Brother before Marriage" in *North American Review*; "The Heaven of Saxophones" in *Passages North*; "Poker Game" in *Poetry Harbor*; "The Center," "Linda," "Stepson," "Chicago," "Poems after the Chinese," "On the Radio," "Flight," and "My Mother at Eighty-Six" in *Tampa Review*; "The Possibility of Love" in *Wisconsin Academy Review*; "Casals" and "'The Azaleas' or 'Azaleas'" in *Transactions of the Wisconsin Academy of Sciences, Arts and Letters*; "Point Arena, California" in *Wisconsin Dialogues*; and "Unexpected Friends" in *Westview*.

A few of these poems appeared in *The Death of the Tenor Sax*, a chapbook from Red Weather Press.

For fellowship support I thank the National Endowment for the Arts, the Minnesota Arts Board, the Ragdale Foundation, and The Tyrone Guthrie Centre.

For one publishing a first collection of poems at age fifty, there are many individuals to thank, too many names for this page and these pages to hold. To teachers, students, and colleagues; friends and family; those who just walked in—my appreciation.

About the Author

A native of Wisconsin, Richard Terrill is the author of three books of creative nonfiction, including *Fakebook: Improvisations on a Journey Back to Jazz* (New York: Limelight Editions, 2000) and *Saturday Night in Baoding: A China Memoir* (University of Arkansas Press, 1990), winner of the Associated Writing Programs Award for nonfiction. He has been awarded fellowships from the National Endowment for the Arts, the Wisconsin and Minnesota State Arts Boards, the Jerome Foundation, and the Bread Loaf Writers' Conference. His essays, poems, and translations from the Chinese have appeared widely in journals such as *North American Review, Iowa Review, Northwest Review, Tampa Review, Michigan Quarterly Review,* and *Fourth Genre.* He has taught at universities in China and Korea, and now teaches creative writing in the MFA program at Minnesota State University, Mankato. He lives in Minneapolis and plays saxophone with local jazz groups.

About the Book

Coming Late to Rachmaninoff is set in Adobe Garamond Pro types based on the sixteenth century roman types of Claude Garamond and the italic types of Robert Granjon. They have been adapted for digital composition by Robert Slimbach in consultation with colleagues including type historian and designer Steven Harvard, letterform expert John Lane, and Adobe's Fred Brady. Slimbach and Brady have written that Garamond's "roman types are arguably the best conceived typefaces ever designed, displaying a superb balance of elegance and practicality." The Granjon italics of the same period are beautiful and graceful companions. The book was designed and typeset by Richard Mathews at the University of Tampa Press. It has been printed on acid-free text papers by Fidlar Doubleday of Kalamazoo, Michigan.

 Poetry from the University of Tampa Press

Jenny Browne, *At Once*

Richard Chess, *Chair in the Desert*

Richard Chess, *Tekiah*

Kathleen Jesme, *Fire Eater*

John Willis Menard, *Lays in Summer Lands*

Jordan Smith, *For Appearances**

Lisa M. Steinman, *Carslaw's Sequences*

Richard Terrill, *Coming Late to Rachmaninoff*

* Denotes winner of the Tampa Review Prize for Poetry

5752